GAMES

FROM BACKGAMMON TO BLACKJACK –
LEARN TO PLAY THE WORLD'S FAVOURITE GAMES

DANIEL KING

KINGFISHER

KINGFISHER

Kingfisher Publications Plc
New Penderel House,
283–288 High Holborn,
London WC1V 7HZ
www.kingfisherpub.com

Author	**Daniel King**
Illustrators	**Julie Hartigan, Mike Buckley**
Managing Editor	**Russell Mclean**
Deputy Art Director	**Mike Buckley**
Senior Production Controller	**Debbie Otter**
DTP Manager	**Nicky Studdart**
Picture Research Manager	**Cee Weston-Baker**
Indexer	**Hilary Bird**

First published by Kingfisher Publications Plc 2003

1 3 5 7 9 10 8 6 4 2

1TR/0503/TEC/MAR(MAR)/128MA

The website addresses listed in this book are correct at the time of going to print. However, due to the ever-changing nature
of the Internet, website addresses and content can change. Websites can contain links that are unsuitable for children. The publisher
cannot be held responsible for changes in website addresses or content, or for information obtained through third-party websites.
We strongly advise that Internet searches should be supervised by an adult.

The publisher would like to thank the following for permission to reproduce their material. Every care has been taken to trace copyright
holders. However, if there have been unintentional omissions or failure to trace copyright holders, we apologise and will, if informed,
endeavour to make corrections in any future edition.

Key: b = bottom, c = centre, l = left, r = right, t = top

4tl Bridgeman / British Museum; **4bl** Bridgeman / Czartoryski Museum, Krakow, Poland; **4** Daniel King; **5tl** www.chessmaster.com; **5tr** Corbis /
Margaret Courtney-Clarke; **5br** Daniel King; **6tl** Bridgeman / Fitzwilliam Museum, University of Cambridge; **6bl** Bridgeman / Vatican Museums
and Galleries, Vatican City; **6–7** Art Archive; **7tr** Art Archive; **7br** Bridgeman / Victoria & Albert Museum; **8tr** British Museum; **8cl** Art Archive /
Turin Museum; **8cr** Corbis / Mimmo Jodice; **8br** AKG / Lobdengau Museum, Landenburg; **9bl** Bridgeman / Royal Asiatic Society, London; **9tr** National
Museum of Ireland, Dublin; **9br** Lady PegLeg; **24tl** British Museum; **30t** British Museum; **31br** Kingfisher plc; **38tl** Topkapi Museum, Istanbul;
38cl www.wopc.co.uk; **38cb** Bridgeman / British Library; **39b** Corbis / Bettmann; **40bl** Bridgeman / Museo Correr, Venice, Italy; **40–41** Corbis /
Angelo Hornak; **41bl** Art Archive / Musée Carnavalet Paris / Dagli Orti; **41cr** Corbis / Bennett Dean; Eye Ubiquitous; **46** Hulton Getty

If you have any comments about this book, please contact the author: dan@danielking.biz

A CIP catalogue record for this book is available from the British Library.

ISBN 0 7534 0816 3

Printed in China

CONTENTS

▲ Our ancestors were just as passionate about board games as we are. This Egyptian board is over 3,000 years old.

◄ Trictrac, a version of backgammon, was popular in Europe for around 400 years. This ornate board was made in Poland in 1584.

INTRODUCTION

Games excite, thrill, amuse and frustrate us. Some people become so fascinated by a game that they devote their lives to understanding it. Games are a central part of our culture. Every day, we use gaming expressions – people talk of political 'stalemate' or someone's 'chequered' career.

Today we can play a vast range of games, on computers or on gaming boards. Most of them are actually versions of far older, highly sophisticated board games that were played by ancient civilizations all over the world.

► In 2002, world chess champion Vladimir Kramnik took on Deep Fritz, the strongest chess computer in the world. The eight-game match was drawn.

MORE THAN A GAME

Throughout the ages, games have been played mainly for amusement and intellectual stimulation. That still holds true today, but they may now be played for other reasons. Games are used as teaching aids in schools, and some people even earn money from playing games.

◀ Computer board games have been a major innovation over the last two decades. Playing against a machine can be a great way to improve your game.

◀ Mancala is mainly played in Africa, but is now recognized around the world as an excellent tool for teaching mathematics.

PROFESSIONAL PLAYERS
Professional games players make their living by competing in tournaments. Whether the game is chess, draughts or go, important title matches are broadcast all over the world on television and through the Internet. In Japan, the strongest go players are celebrities. The top matches receive enormous coverage all over the Far East.

INTERNET INFLUENCE
The Internet has breathed new life into many ancient games, allowing people from all over the world to play against each other, online and in real time. It has popularized games such as go and mancala that were traditionally played only in a particular part of the world.

GAMES FOR LIFE
Games play an important role in education – just like in life, we must learn to play by certain rules; we cannot undo our actions, but must learn to accept responsibility; we learn how being creative can bring success; we learn how to analyze our strategy and our actions, and improve on them for the next occasion. And games teach us perhaps the hardest lesson of all – how to accept defeat and victory with equal measure.

▼ Dama, or Turkish draughts, is a popular board game throughout the Middle East.

▲ The Ancient Egyptian game of mehen was played on a snake-shaped board. It dates back to 3000 BCE. A version of mehen is still played in the Sudan.

ANCIENT GAMES I

Some board games are so perfectly formed that we can only imagine them to be the invention of one person. Many myths support this view. It is said that the Chinese game of go (also known as wei-chi) was invented by the Emperor Yao around 2200 BCE to strengthen the mind of his degenerate son, Shokin.

THE MYTH OF THE FOOLISH KING
Chess is supposed to have been invented by a vizier, or minister, to an Indian king. The king was so impressed by the game that he offered his vizier a reward. The vizier asked for a grain of rice on the first square of the chess board, two grains of rice on the second square, four grains on the third square, eight on the next square, and so on, doubling the number of grains until all 64 squares were filled. The king readily agreed to such a humble reward, but soon realized there was not enough rice in the kingdom to satisfy the request. The king had been made to look a fool, and the vizier was beheaded.

▲ This wine pitcher from around 540 BCE shows the Ancient Greek heroes Ajax and Achilles in intellectual combat over a board game.

▶ These Roman dice and gaming counters are made from bone. Their design varies little from those we use today for games such as backgammon.

HOW GAMES REALLY BEGAN

From around 12,000 years ago, humans began to gather together in communities. They lived in houses, harvested crops and traded their surplus goods with other villages. They had more security than their ancestors – nomads who wandered the land in search of food – and were able to spend time away from work. Playing games became the perfect way of filling these periods of leisure.

FROM RELIGION TO RACING

Archaeologists have found evidence of board games dating back to the earliest civilizations of the Middle East, India and China. Many games appear to have developed from religious ceremonies in which an early type of die was thrown to divine the future. It is easy to imagine how this led to counters being used to keep a tally of the scores, and how the moving counters could be likened to racing athletes or horses.

These 'race games' are the most ancient board games we know of, and were played by cultures all over the world. They are still the most common type of game – snakes and ladders, ludo and backgammon all involve racing counters around a board, and all three have ancient roots.

▲ *Backgammon was highly popular in medieval Europe. This illustration is from the famous* Book of Games, *written in 1282 for Alfonso the Wise, King of Castile (an area in present-day Spain).*

▶ *This 19th-century print shows two Japanese go players in heated competition. To be successful at board games, however, it is best to control your emotions and remain cool.*

ANCIENT GAMES II

The origins of race games such as backgammon probably lie in the ancient cultures of the Middle East. The oldest complete gaming board was discovered in the royal graves of Ur, an ancient city in Sumer (an area that is now southern Iraq).

▲ *The royal game of Ur dates back to around 2500 BCE. Each player raced seven counters around the board, their moves determined by pyramid-shaped dice. The game was probably played in the Middle East for over 2,000 years. Boards have been found scratched into temple floors from a much later period, and the rules were discovered on a tablet dated 176 BCE.*

▶ *Played by the Ancient Egyptians, senet was a race game similar to the royal game of Ur. Judging by the number of boards found in tombs and depicted in paintings, senet, and related games such as the game of twenty, were an important part of Egyptian culture.*

CULTURAL CONTACT

The discovery of similar board games around the world reveals that, even thousands of years ago, diverse cultures were coming into contact with each other, and sharing ideas and customs. For example, the distinctive nine men's morris board (see pages 10–11) has been discovered at the very western end of Europe, in Ireland, but also all over Asia.

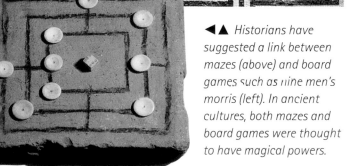

◀▲ *Historians have suggested a link between mazes (above) and board games such as nine men's morris (left). In ancient cultures, both mazes and board games were thought to have magical powers.*

MANCALA ON THE MOVE

Another game which spread far and wide is mancala (see pages 30–33). Its origins are African, but it is now played over much of the globe. The Arabs took the game along their trading routes into Asia – versions of mancala have been found in China, Sri Lanka and the Philippines. African slaves carried the game west to the Americas.

CHANGING CHESS

From its beginnings in central Asia, chess travelled far to the east and west. The game changed little by little, to improve play or just to suit the particular culture that played it. In the east, China and Japan have their own forms of chess that are just as ancient as the western – and now international – form of the game.

Unfortunately, chess and backgammon became so popular across Europe in the Middle Ages that other games were neglected. For example, hnefatafl was popular throughout the Viking world (Scandinavia, Iceland and parts of Britain and Ireland) for over 700 years until around CE 1100.

▶ This hnefatafl board dates from the 10th century CE. It was discovered in Ballinderry, Ireland. A king was placed in the centre, protected by dark-coloured guards. Around the outside of the board stood light-coloured attackers whose goal was to capture the king. The king's aim, with the aid of its guards, was to find a safe path to the side of the board.

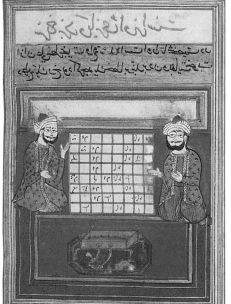

◀ The Arabs were the first people to make a serious study of chess. This illustration is from a 14th-century manuscript.

FROM ALQUERQUE TO DRAUGHTS

Another effect of the popularity of chess was that other games were transferred on to a chequered board. Draughts, for example, derives from alquerque, a far older game than chess.

◀ Alquerque pieces were placed on the intersecting points of this net-like grid. When people began to play the game on a chess board, the pieces were placed in the squares but the diagonal movements remained.

NINE MEN'S MORRIS

Nine men's morris has been played for thousands of years by cultures all over the world, from Ancient Egypt to China, from Troy to Neolithic Ireland.

The reason for the game's long popularity lies in its simple form. You can scratch the shape of a board in the earth, pick up some pebbles and play. Nine men's morris is best described as a complicated version of noughts and crosses. One of your aims is to form a line of three men. This allows you to permanently remove one of your opponent's pieces from the board.

Did you know?

The word 'morris' has nothing to do with the old English dance of the same name. It comes from the Latin word merellus, *which means a counter or gaming piece. Nine men's morris was one of many board games played by the Romans.*

Black's move has blocked White's attempt to form a row of three.

1

MOVING AND WINNING

There are two ways to win – by blocking your opponent's pieces so that they cannot move, or by leaving your opponent with just two men, making it impossible to form a line of three.

The game falls into two phases. In phase one, the two players take turns to place their nine men on the board, one by one. Men are placed on the points where lines intersect **(diagram 1)**.

Black moves a man, ready to form a line of three on the next turn.

2

After all 18 men have been placed on the board, phase two begins. The players manoeuvre their pieces, still taking turns, and try to form a line of three. Men are moved one step along the lines to the next point, as long as it is vacant **(diagram 2)**.

THREE IN A ROW

If you manage to make a row of three men along a straight line, you can remove any one of your opponent's pieces as long as it is not part of a line of three. A piece from a line of three can be captured only if no other men are available.

The line of three cannot be used to take another enemy piece on your next turn. First, one of your three men must move away, and then roll back into position on the turn after. Be careful that your opponent does not block the line when you move away. If you are skilful enough, you might be able to create a lethal formation – two rolling lines of three (diagram 3).

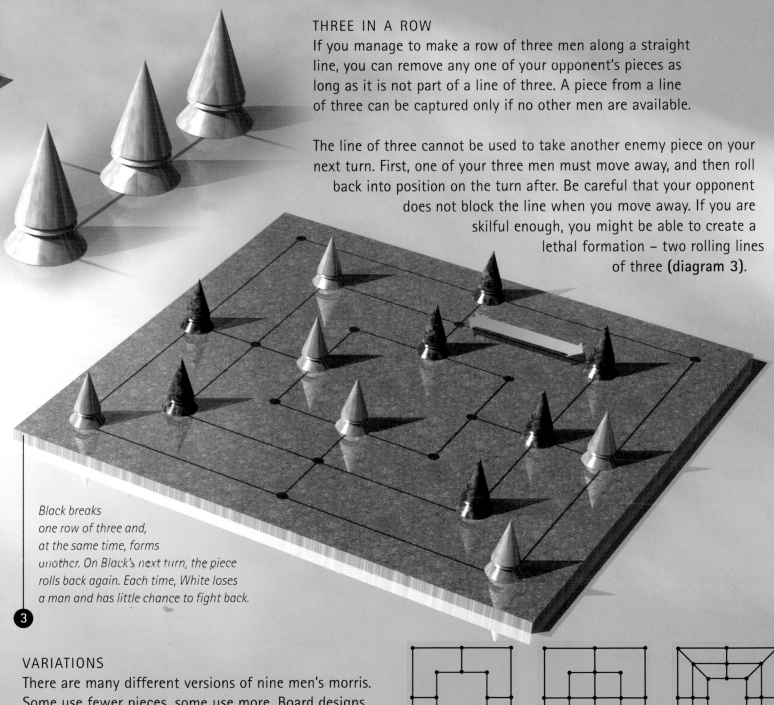

Black breaks one row of three and, at the same time, forms another. On Black's next turn, the piece rolls back again. Each time, White loses a man and has little chance to fight back.

3

VARIATIONS

There are many different versions of nine men's morris. Some use fewer pieces, some use more. Board designs vary too. Try out these versions to see which you like best. Rules are essentially the same as for the nine man game – forming a row of three is the objective.

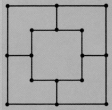

Five men's morris

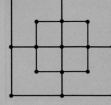

Seven men's morris

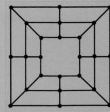

Twelve men's morris

FOX AND GEESE

Fox and geese is a 'chase' game. The two sides have unequal powers and different aims. The pack of geese must trap the fox so that it cannot move, but the fox will win the game if it remains free. Fox and geese is a test of nerves. If the geese rush forwards too quickly they will be doomed, while the lone fox must wait patiently for the geese to show weakness.

SETTING UP

The 13 geese are arranged as shown below. The fox starts on any empty point, but somewhere near the centre is best. This allows the fox to cover all sides of the board. The player with the geese makes the first move, then the two sides take it in turns.

▼ *Fox and geese is played on a round or cross-shaped board. The 13 geese (red) are placed at one end of the board and the single fox (blue) is usually placed near the centre.*

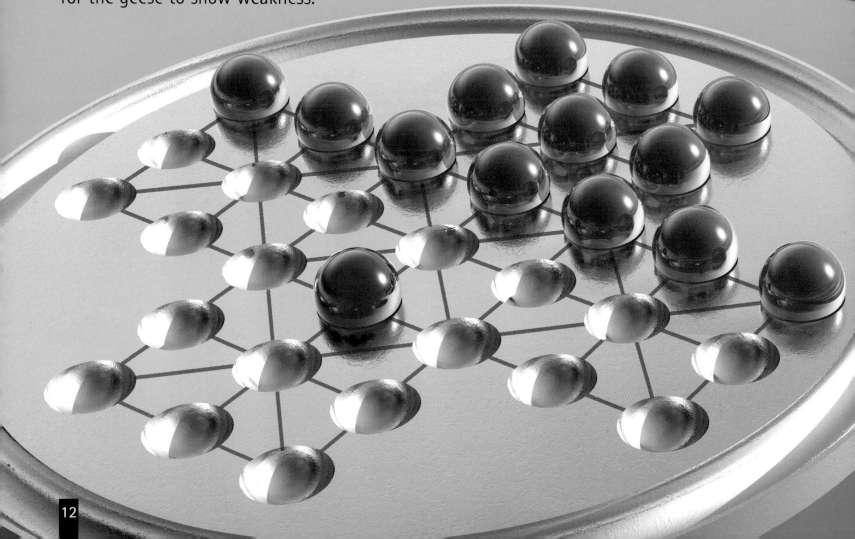

MOVING

Fox and geese is easiest to play on a board with lines that show where the pieces are allowed to move. A goose may move one space at a time in any direction (forwards, backwards, sideways or diagonally) to the nearest empty point, but only along the lines **(diagram 1)**. Geese cannot jump over each other or the fox. The fox moves in the same way along the lines, but is able to capture geese by leaping over them **(diagram 2)**.

1

Here, the goose in the centre could move directly forwards, forwards along the diagonals, or to either side. Going forwards would not be a good idea – the piece could be taken. It would be better to move up one of the geese from the pack, as shown.

The fox captures a goose by leaping over it along a straight line to an unoccupied point on the other side. More than one goose may be captured in a single move.

2

STRATEGY

The geese must work together, protecting each other from capture. Try not to let a goose be separated from the pack, or the fox could hunt it down. Edge up the board slowly, gradually restricting the fox's territory. At the start of the game, several geese at the back of the pack will not be involved. Try to bring them into the game as soon as possible – only by using all the geese can you hope to trap the fox.

If you are the fox, remember that you cannot be captured – so if you spy an opening in the pack, slip into it. It is almost impossible to be trapped in the centre of the board, so the fox can make daring raids without risk. Attack lone geese – even if you cannot force a capture, keeping the geese busy with defence will frustrate their plans.

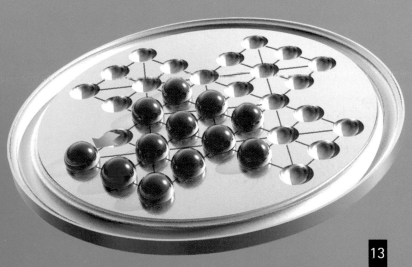

▶ *With this last move, the geese have trapped the fox and won the game.*

BACKGAMMON

Backgammon is fast-moving and treacherous. Two players race counters around the board – the first to guide them home and out is the winner. Although this is a game of great strategic skill, the rules are relatively simple.

THE AIM
The aim in backgammon is to remove all your pieces from the board before your opponent. To do this, you must bring the counters into the 'home board'.

SETTING UP
Each player begins with 15 pieces. One side has white, the other black. The pieces are always set up in the same way at the start of the game.

Black sits here

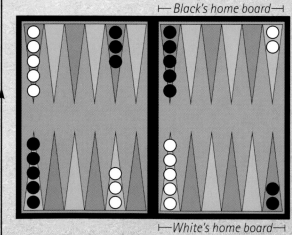

White moves in this direction

⊢— *Black's home board* —⊣

◄► *The pieces are placed on 'points'. On many boards the points are alternately coloured, but that has no bearing on the game. These two diagrams show how the board looks at the start of a game.*

⊢—*White's home board*—⊣

⊢—*Black moves in this direction* —⊣

BEGINNING THE GAME
Each player throws a die. The player with the higher score begins, using the scores from both dice. After that, the players take it in turns to move, rolling two dice at a time.

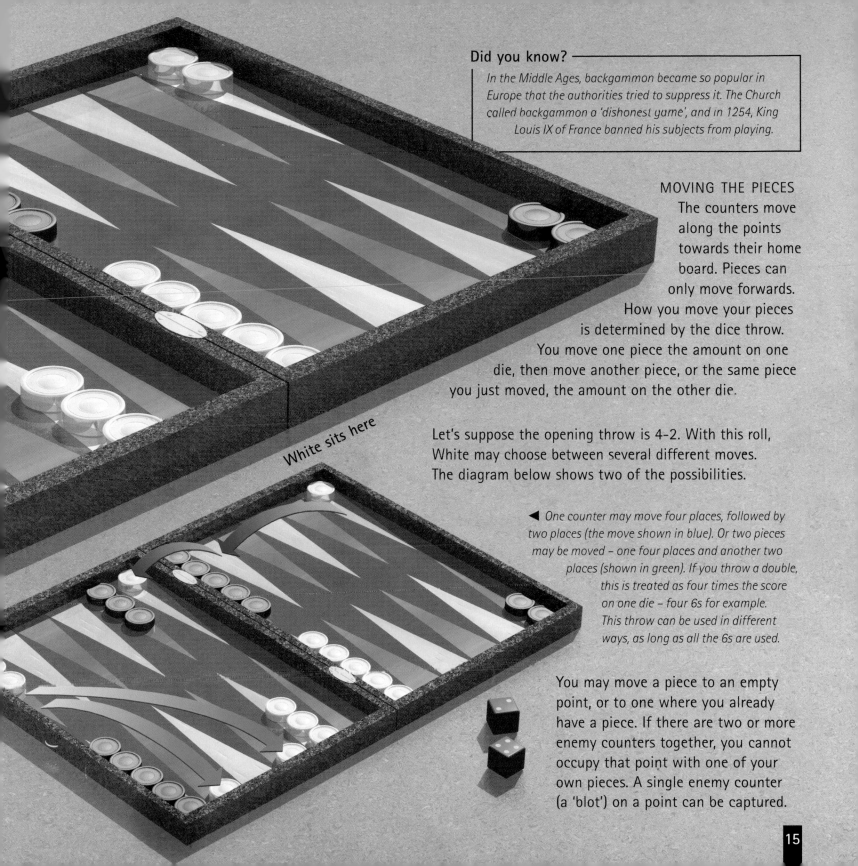

Did you know?

In the Middle Ages, backgammon became so popular in Europe that the authorities tried to suppress it. The Church called backgammon a 'dishonest game', and in 1254, King Louis IX of France banned his subjects from playing.

MOVING THE PIECES

The counters move along the points towards their home board. Pieces can only move forwards. How you move your pieces is determined by the dice throw. You move one piece the amount on one die, then move another piece, or the same piece you just moved, the amount on the other die.

Let's suppose the opening throw is 4-2. With this roll, White may choose between several different moves. The diagram below shows two of the possibilities.

White sits here

◀ *One counter may move four places, followed by two places (the move shown in blue). Or two pieces may be moved – one four places and another two places (shown in green). If you throw a double, this is treated as four times the score on one die – four 6s for example. This throw can be used in different ways, as long as all the 6s are used.*

You may move a piece to an empty point, or to one where you already have a piece. If there are two or more enemy counters together, you cannot occupy that point with one of your own pieces. A single enemy counter (a 'blot') on a point can be captured.

HITS, BLOTS AND BEARING OFF

When a backgammon counter is captured (or 'hit') it does not leave the board for good. It sits on the central bar before returning into play via the opponent's home board.

Hitting plays an important role in backgammon – it slows up your opponent, as a captured counter must re-start the journey back to its own home board (diagrams 1–3).

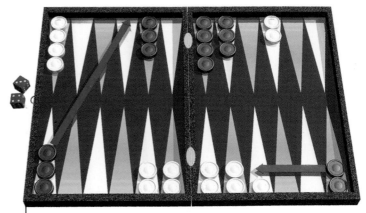

In this position, a throw of 4-3 allows Black to use the 3 to hit White's unprotected blot (a single counter). The two White counters next to it are safe, so Black must use the 4 in another way, as shown.

1

— Black's home board —

2 *After being hit, the White counter is placed on the bar – the central ridge of the board. Before White can make any other move, this counter must re-enter the game via Black's home board.*

6 5 4 3 2 1

3

When you return a counter to the board, imagine that the points are numbered from one to six. Suppose White now throws 5-2. The five-point is already occupied by Black counters, but the two-point is vacant – so the White counter returns on the two-point and the 5 is used elsewhere. If White had thrown a double 5 or a double 6, the counter would not have been able to return to the board and the turn would have passed to Black.

If one side has several counters on the bar, they must all re-enter the opponent's home board before any other counters are able to move.

FINISHING THE GAME

The first player to remove (or 'bear off') all their counters from the board wins the game. Before bearing off can begin, a player must move their counters into the home board (**diagrams 4 and 5**).

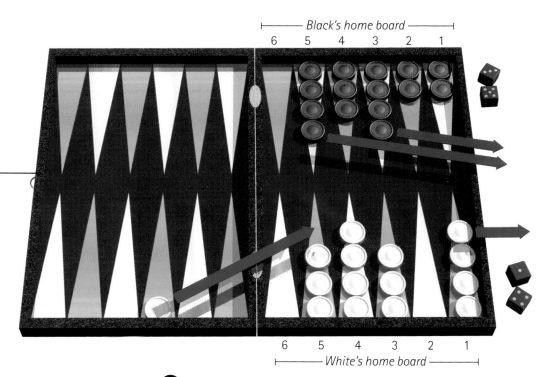

With all the Black counters inside the home board, Black is ready to begin bearing off. If Black throws 5-3, two counters can be removed – one from the five-point and one from the three-point.

White is behind in the race. Before bearing off can begin, one last counter must be brought into the home board. Suppose White rolls 4-1. The last counter is brought inside the home board with the 4, and the 1 is used to bear off a counter from the one-point. The race is on.

Black's next throw is a double 6 – a great stroke of luck. Remember, a double gives you four times the score on one die, so Black has four 6s to use. The six-point is empty, so Black bears off from the next point down – three counters are removed from the five-point. The five-point is now empty, so the final 6 is used to bear off a counter from the four-point.

White is less lucky with a roll of 6-2. As we have seen, the 6 can be used to bear off a counter from the five-point, but the two-point is empty. White cannot bear off from the one-point, as there are still counters above the two-point. Instead, White uses the 2 to fill the gap on the two-point, making sure that two counters will bear off on the next throw.

Let's take stock. Black has taken off six counters, White has only removed two. Black will probably win the race, but if White were to throw a couple of doubles, the game could still swing round.

POINTS AND PRIMES

The ultimate aim in backgammon is to bear off your pieces before your opponent. This might lead you to think that strategy is simple – you charge your counters around the board, and the dice decide who crosses the finishing line first. In fact, a straight race is very rare. The best backgammon players combine the efficient movement of their own counters with the restriction of their opponent's pieces.

BUILDING SECURE POINTS

We have already seen that hitting your opponent's pieces is one way to slow down their progress, but that depends on the luck of the dice. Another way is to create secure points around the board.

Suppose White's opening dice roll is 6-1. This is one of the most useful rolls at the start of the game, as it allows White to 'build' (occupy) the important seven-point **(diagram 1)**. Building secure points not only limits your opponent's mobility, but also provides safe stepping stones for your own counters on the perilous journey back to the home board.

THE SIX-POINT PRIME

The six-point prime is a highly effective blocking strategy, formed by building six secure points in a row **(diagram 2)**.

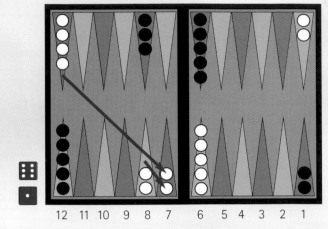

12 11 10 9 8 7 | 6 5 4 3 2 1

1 *With an opening roll of 6-1, White occupies the seven-point. Sooner or later, Black's two back counters (on the one-point) must make a run back to their own home board. That becomes harder when there is a barrier to leap over.*

Here, White has built a six-point prime. Black's two back counters are unable to leap over White's six secure points, so they are trapped. Over the next few moves, White leaves the blocking 'prime' in position and brings the rest of the counters into the home board. Even if the two Black counters in the corner do finally escape (after White brings the two counters on the seven-point into the home board), then White will be way ahead in the race to bear off.

THE GOLDEN POINT

How can you prevent your two back counters from becoming blockaded? Charging both pieces around the board to safety is a risky strategy. Even if one piece makes it, the other could be stranded, then hit and blocked by incoming enemy counters. An alternative tactic is to secure a foothold further up in your opponent's home board – on the five-point, for example **(diagrams 3 and 4)**. Thanks to its strategic importance, the five-point is known as the golden point.

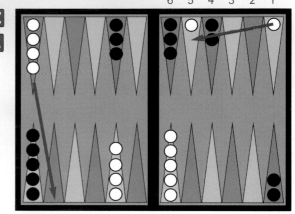

3 *Here, White has already moved one of the back counters up to the five-point. White now rolls 4-2 and uses the 4 to occupy the five-point. From here it is easier for White's two back counters to make a break for safety. They are also in a good position to hit stray Black blots, and they provide a safe point for other White counters returning from the bar.*

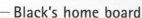
— Black's home board —

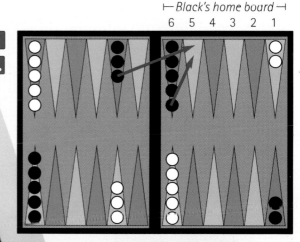

4 *If your opening roll is 3-1, occupy the golden point in your home board. Not only is it the first step in restricting your opponent's back counters, but it prevents them building on the five-point themselves.*

— White's home board —

Go

The game of go has an appealing purity. One side plays with white stones, the other with black. The opposing forces attempt to surround each other in a subtle struggle. A game of chess or draughts can be won by a lightning attack, but to do well at go you must have patience and a cool overview of the board.

CHINESE ORIGINS

The game began in China, possibly as long ago as 2000 BCE. Ancient texts describe the board in astrological terms, suggesting that go developed from a way of predicting the future from the stars.

The Japanese took go to a new level of sophistication in the period of the Tokugawa shoguns, or warrior rulers (1603–1867). Schools were set up to develop the theory of the game, which was thought to provide excellent moral, intellectual and strategic training.

GLOBAL GO

Go is now played all over the world, although it is most popular in China, Japan and Korea. In Japan there are over 400 professional players. Go has a ranking system similar to that of karate – apprentice professionals start at 1-dan and try to work their way up to the highest title of 9-dan.

▼ Go is a game for two players. Tournament games are played on a board of 19 horizontal and 19 vertical lines. The black dots act as markers to help players judge where to lay their stones.

Tip

Games on a full-size board are fascinating, but can last a long time. To start with, play on a small board of 9 x 9 lines (use a chess board, and place stones on the lines rather than in the squares). The rules are the same as on a large board, and it is a good way to develop your strategies.

STARTING THE GAME

The board is empty at the start of the game. Black has 181 stones, White has 180 stones – although it is very rare that all of them are used. Stones are not placed in the squares, but on the points where lines intersect. Black always plays first, then the players take turns. Once a stone is placed, it cannot be moved, but it can be captured.

THE AIM

The aim in go is to surround a greater amount of territory than your opponent. The game ends when both players feel they cannot gain any more territory or capture any more stones. Players score one point for each empty intersection inside their own territory, and one point for every stone they have captured. The player with the larger total is the winner.

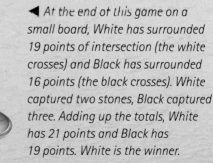

◄ *At the end of this game on a small board, White has surrounded 19 points of intersection (the white crosses) and Black has surrounded 16 points (the black crosses). White captured two stones, Black captured three. Adding up the totals, White has 21 points and Black has 19 points. White is the winner.*

LIBERTIES, GROUPS AND EYES

Although the chief aim in go is to surround as much territory as possible, capturing enemy stones may help you to achieve that goal. Captured stones also count towards your score at the end of the game.

LIBERTIES

A stone in the middle of the board has four open points around it. These are called liberties **(diagram 1)**. To capture that stone, enemy stones must occupy all four points **(diagram 2)**.

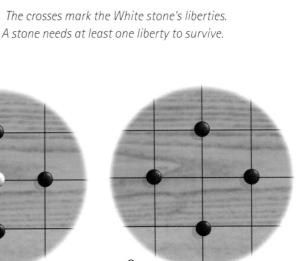

1 *The crosses mark the White stone's liberties. A stone needs at least one liberty to survive.*

2 *Here, three of the White stone's liberties have been taken (A). To capture the White stone, Black places a stone on the final liberty (B). The White stone is removed from the board (C).*

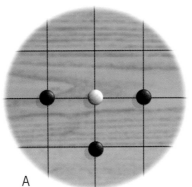

A

B

C

Stones can also be captured at the sides and in the corners of the board **(diagrams 3 and 4)**.

3 *At the side of the board, a stone has only three liberties. Black captures the White stone by playing a stone as shown.*

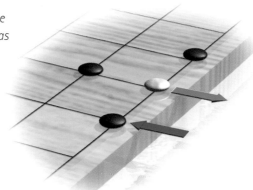

4 *In the corner, a stone has only two liberties. Placing a Black stone as shown captures the White stone in the corner.*

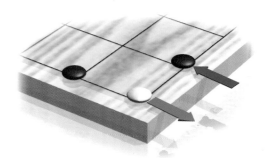

GROUPS

Forming groups of stones can be a good way to enclose territory and protect your stones. A group of stones can be captured, but to do so, the entire group must be surrounded and all its liberties closed (diagrams 5–7).

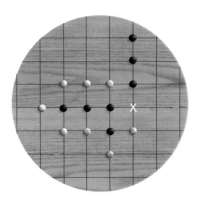

5 *In this position, the point marked with a cross is particularly important. It is called the 'cutting point'.*

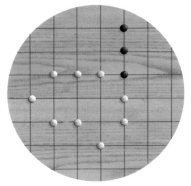

6 *If White is to play, placing a stone on the cutting point surrounds and captures the group of four Black stones.*

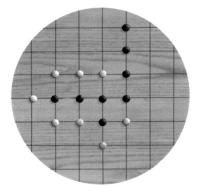

7 *A Black stone laid on the cutting point forms a strong chain. With several isolated stones, White is now in the weaker position.*

EYES

In order to create a completely secure group of stones, that group must enclose two vacant points, or 'eyes' (diagram 8). A group with just one eye is vulnerable to capture (diagram 9).

9 *A group with one eye is not secure. Here, it would be legal for White to place a stone on the eye in the middle of the Black group. Again, the White stone will be surrounded by Black stones, but this time the move will close off the Black group's last liberty. The Black stones will be captured.*

8 *Here, the Black stones are safe from capture because the group contains two eyes (marked with crosses). It is illegal for White to place a stone on either of the two eyes, as that stone would have no liberties.*

STRATEGY

In professional games, the struggle often revolves around the corners. Diagram 10 illustrates why.

10 *Each group of stones encloses the same amount of territory – nine points. In the middle, twelve stones are needed to do this. At the side, it is nine stones. In the corner, only six stones are required. In other words, territory can be enclosed most efficiently in the corners of the board.*

Test position
Solution on pages 60–61

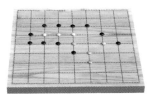

How can Black, to play, capture five White stones? Think a few moves ahead to find the answer.

CHESS

▲ *The Isle of Lewis chess pieces date from the 12th century. Carved from walrus ivory, they form the oldest surviving complete set.*

Chess is a game of war in which the fate of your army depends entirely on your own skill. In other games, moves may be determined by a roll of the dice or the turn of a card. But luck plays no part in chess. This, combined with the game's complexity, explains why chess can be one of the most satisfying of all games to win.

CHESS ON THE MOVE

Chess first emerged in northern India, before spreading to the Arab world. By the Middle Ages it had become the most popular game in Europe. Chess is now played worldwide by millions of people. The number of players continues to grow with the popularity of chess-playing sites on the Internet.

| Rook | Knight | Bishop | King | Queen | Pawn |

▲ *In chess diagrams, each piece is represented by a symbol. Don't muddle up king and queen – the king is the taller of the two pieces and has a cross on top.*

SETTING UP

Chess is played by two players on a board of 64 squares. Half of the squares are white (or a pale colour) and the other half black (or a dark colour). One player commands the white pieces, the other the black, and they take it in turns to move. White always makes the first move.

At the beginning of the game, position the board so that there is a white square at the bottom right-hand corner. Then set up the pieces. On the first row of squares (or 'rank') stand the most important pieces. The rooks sit in the corners. Next to them on both sides of the board are the knights. Then come the bishops and finally, on the middle two squares, stand the queen and king.

Be sure to put the king and queen on the correct squares. There is an easy rule to help you – the queen stands on its own colour. In other words, if you have a White queen, place it on the white square nearest the middle. If you have a Black queen, stand it on the black square nearest the middle. In front of these pieces, on the second rank, is a row of eight pawns.

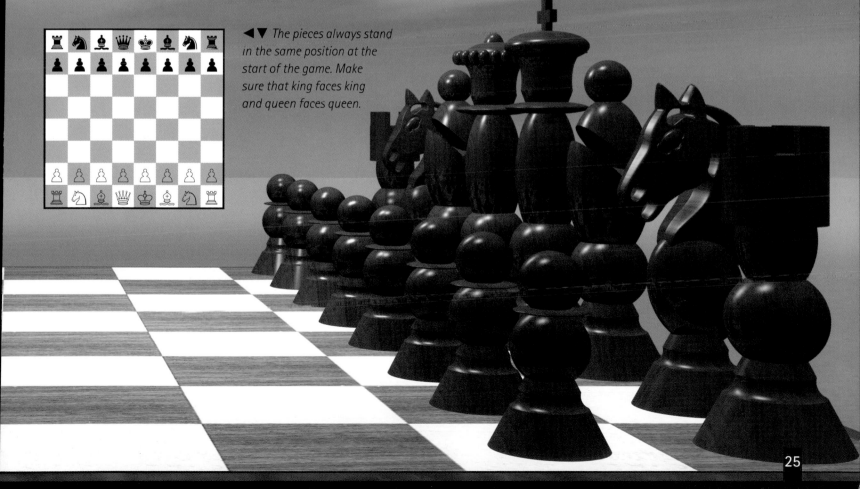

◀▼ *The pieces always stand in the same position at the start of the game. Make sure that king faces king and queen faces queen.*

THE PIECES

The best way to learn how the pieces move is to practise with them on a clear chess board. Take the pieces one at a time, mastering each one's unique movement, before starting a full game.

1

THE KING ♔

The king is the tallest chess piece. The whole game revolves around the struggle to trap the king into checkmate (see pages 28–29). That makes it the most important piece on the board, but the king is actually one of the least powerful. It moves one square at a time, although this can be in any direction.

2

THE BISHOP ♗

A bishop may move forwards or backwards along the diagonals for as many squares as it likes, as long as there is nothing standing in the way. Both armies have two bishops – one runs along the dark squares of the board, the other along the light squares.

THE ROOK ♖

The rook is a powerful piece, moving in a straight line up and down and from side to side for as many squares as it likes – unless something is blocking its path. Rooks cannot leap over other pieces, apart from when they perform the special move of castling (see page 27).

3

4 *THE QUEEN* ♕

The queen has a crown at the top of the piece, and is a little shorter than the king, which it stands next to at the start of battle. The queen is the most powerful piece on the board. It moves up and down and from side to side across the board like a rook, as well as along the diagonals like a bishop, provided nothing is blocking its path.

5

THE KNIGHT ♘

The knight moves in an L shape – two squares in a straight line and then one to the left or right. The knight makes the game more dynamic. In positions that appear blocked it can force a breakthrough, because it is the only piece that can leap over other pieces. Here, for example, the knight in the corner can capture the bishop on the other side of the pawns.

6

THE PAWN ♙

On its first move, a pawn may advance either two squares or one (A). After this, it can only move forwards one square at a time (B). Pawns capture in a different way to how they normally move – by advancing one square diagonally forwards. Here, for example, the pawn in front of the rook and the knight could take either piece (C). If a pawn reaches the far side of the board, it changes into a rook, knight, bishop or queen (D). Most players choose a queen, as it is the most powerful piece on the board.

SPECIAL MOVES – CASTLING

Castling is a good way to protect your king and also move a powerful piece, the rook, into battle. In short castling, the king moves two squares towards the nearest rook. The rook leaps over the king, landing next to it. In long castling, the king moves two squares towards the farthest rook. The rook jumps over the king and lands next to it. There are a few rules to remember – you cannot castle if your king or rook has already moved, if your king is in check, if your king will land into a check, or if a piece is standing between the king and rook.

Short castling

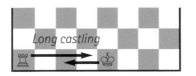

Long castling

SPECIAL MOVES – EN PASSANT

This special method of pawn capture is only available in a particular situation. When a pawn advances two squares from its starting position, an enemy pawn standing next to it on the fifth rank may capture it. In this example, the White pawn moves one square diagonally behind the Black pawn and removes it from the board. It is as if the Black pawn had only moved one square. An 'en passant' capture must be made on the turn immediately after the enemy pawn has moved two squares, or the option disappears.

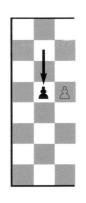

Did you know?

Many players like to announce 'check', but under the rules of the game, it is not necessary to do so. Often a player says it just to rattle the opponent!

White's king is under attack from the rook. We say that the king is in check. The king must move out of check at once. The only option is to move forwards one square.

1

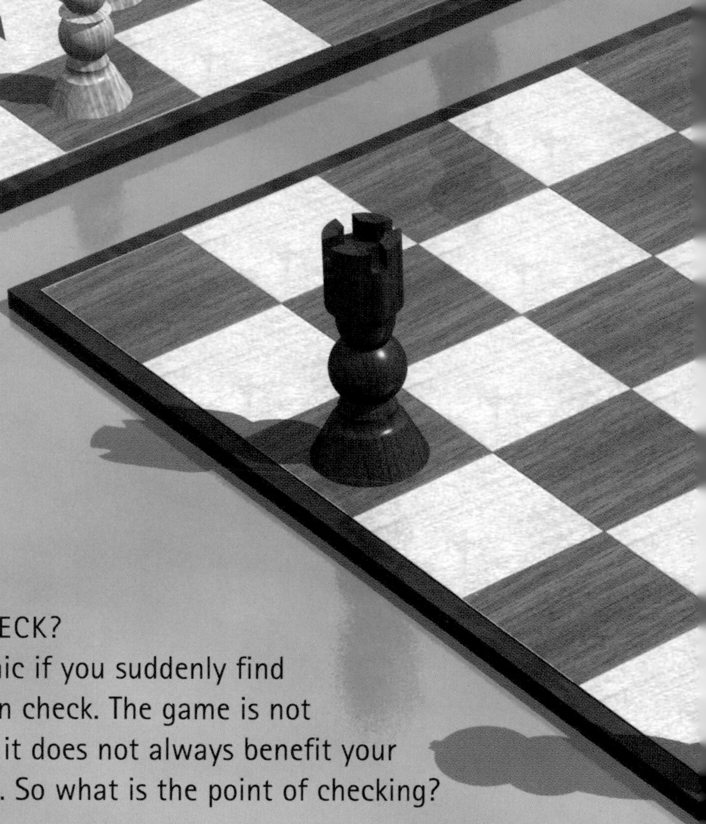

Board Games – Chess

CHECK AND CHECKMATE

The ultimate aim in a game of chess is to checkmate your opponent's king. The term comes from the ancient Persian *shah mat*, which means 'the king is defeated'.

To reach checkmate, you must threaten the enemy king with one of your pieces so that the king is unable to move and escape capture. Normally, a checkmate occurs when one side has an overwhelming superiority in forces, or through a direct and unexpected assault on the king.

Checking occurs when the king is attacked but can still escape. In other words, it is not fatal. Diagrams 1 and 2 demonstrate what the terms mean.

WHY CHECK?

Don't panic if you suddenly find yourself in check. The game is not over, and it does not always benefit your opponent. So what is the point of checking?

• A check can help to gain time.

• Checking can drive the enemy king to a poor square, leaving it open to further attack.

TEST POSITIONS

To make sure you understand the concepts of check and checkmate, here are two test positions to solve. Work out whether it is check or checkmate, and if it is only check, how do you escape? The solutions are on pages 60–61.

Test position

(White to play)
Is this check or checkmate?

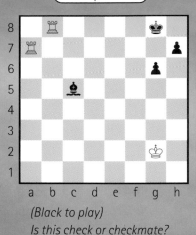

Test position

(Black to play)
Is this check or checkmate?

White's king is again in check from the rook, but this time there is no escape. The king is trapped by its own pawns and cannot move out of check, so we say it is checkmated. The game is over and Black has won!

②

Did you know?

If you fail to spot that you are in check, and do not prevent the attack to your king, it does not mean you lose the game. Your opponent has to let you retake your move to get out of check.

STALEMATE

This is when a player cannot make any legal moves, but is not in check. It usually occurs when one army has an overwhelming advantage and is moving in for a checkmate against an exposed king **(diagram 3)**.

With a king and queen against a lone Black king, White aims for a swift checkmate. The queen closes in for the kill, but comes too close. Black's king has no legal moves, but is not checkmated. This position is stalemate and the game is drawn.

③

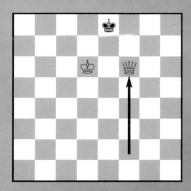

29

MANCALA

Mancala is the most popular board game in Africa. It is a game of pure skill. To do well you must be quick-witted and able to think ahead for many moves.

In African communities, mancala is a social game. Spectators often join in, suggesting or even making moves. Mancala is fiendishly complicated, so you can spend a long time thinking over each position, trying to calculate all the different possibilities. But in Africa, play is traditionally fast and furious.

▲ *Although a mancala board can be made very easily, many boards are expertly carved. This board in the shape of a wheelbarrow is from Sierra Leone, in Africa.*

Large hole to store beans captured by player two

Player two sits here

Player one sits here

BOARDS AND BEANS
Mancala boards are usually carved from wood, but a simple board can be made by scooping out holes from sand or earth. The playing pieces are made of almost anything, as long as they are roughly the same size and pleasant to hold – nuts, beans, pebbles or shells, for example. In other words, with a little resourcefulness, you can play mancala anywhere.

SETTING UP
The two players sit either side of the board. Each of the 12 holes is filled with four beans, making 48 beans in all. A larger cup at each end is for storing captured beans. Players take it in turns to move.

THE AIM
The aim in mancala is to win the most beans, so when one player has won more than half the beans (25+), the game finishes. If both players win 24 beans, the game is a draw.

Large hole to store beans captured by player one

MOVING

To begin the game, a player scoops up all the beans from any hole on their side of the board. Starting from the next hole on the right, the beans are dropped one at a time into each hole in an anticlockwise direction, sowing on the opponent's side of the board as well. When all four beans have been distributed, the turn finishes. Players take it in turns to sow beans in this way.

▲ *Here, player one has started the game by scooping four beans from the second hole on the right.*

▶ *From ancient to modern – some mobile phones now feature a version of mancala.*

CAPTURING BEANS

To make a capture in mancala, you must finish sowing on your opponent's side of the board, in a hole that contains just one or two beans (making the total two or three beans after the sowing).

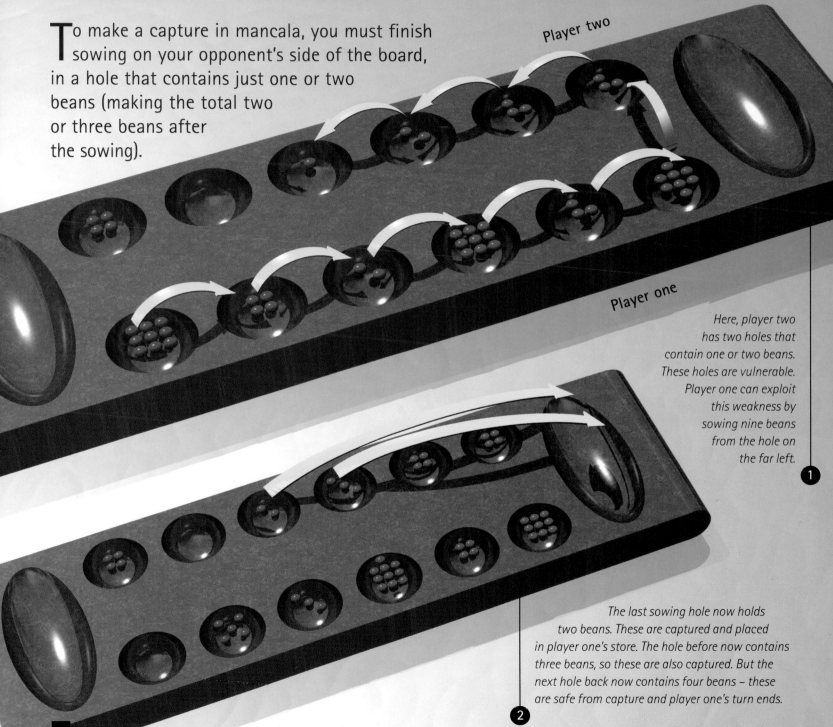

Player two

Player one

Here, player two has two holes that contain one or two beans. These holes are vulnerable. Player one can exploit this weakness by sowing nine beans from the hole on the far left.

1

The last sowing hole now holds two beans. These are captured and placed in player one's store. The hole before now contains three beans, so these are also captured. But the next hole back now contains four beans – these are safe from capture and player one's turn ends.

2

MANCALA RULES

If you sow from a hole containing 12 or more beans, you will make a full circuit of the board. When you reach the hole you started from, skip over it and continue sowing at the next hole.

If there are no beans left on your opponent's side of the board, you must, if possible, sow beans on to that side so that your opponent can make a move on the next turn.

If there are just a few beans left on the board and it is clear that no further captures can be made, the game is stopped. The remaining beans are not counted, and the player with the largest number of beans in their store is the winner.

Player two

Player one

Although player two has no holes containing one or two beans, player one can create targets with a massive lap of the board. Fifteen beans are scooped from the hole on the far right. Remember that a bean cannot be sown into the hole from which it was originally scooped.

3

4

Player one's circuit of the board has created pots of two in the previously empty holes. Player one captures the beans from four holes.

STRATEGY

As we have seen, leaving one or two beans in a hole on your side of the board can be dangerous. If that happens, sow the beans on or sow into the hole to create a greater number. A good strategy is to build up a large number of beans in one of your holes. If you time it right, sowing them around the board can be an effective way to attack (**diagrams 3 and 4**).

Test positions

Solutions on pages 60–61

What move should player two make?

What move should player one make?

33

DRAUGHTS

Draughts is one of the most underrated games in the world. Because it is played on the same chequered board, it is often assumed to be an inferior version of chess. But the games are very different, and draughts is far more complex than its simple rules suggest.

THE AIM

One way to win a game of draughts is to capture all your opponent's pieces (checkers). Another way is to immobilize them – in other words, if you make a move but your opponent cannot, you win the game.

Sometimes it is possible to capture several pieces on one turn. Here, the Black checker can leap over and capture two enemy pieces.

1

▶ *The board is placed with a white square in the bottom right-hand corner. Each side has 12 pieces, which are placed on the dark squares. Black always begins and players take it in turns to move.*

MOVING AND CAPTURING

The pieces may move one square diagonally forwards to the left or right – but they cannot move backwards. A checker captures an enemy piece by leaping over it and occupying the space diagonally the other side **(diagram 1)**. When a piece is captured, it is removed from the board. If you can take ('jump') a piece, then you must do so.

KINGS

When a piece reaches the end of the board, it automatically becomes a king, and the player's move finishes. The piece is crowned by placing a checker of the same colour on top of it **(diagram 2)**. Kings move and capture in the same way as single pieces, but they may do so by going both forwards and backwards. This makes them far more powerful than ordinary checkers.

Did you know?

Draughts has been played in Europe since the end of the 1100s, but it is probably descended from a far older game, alquerque, which dates back thousands of years to Ancient Egypt.

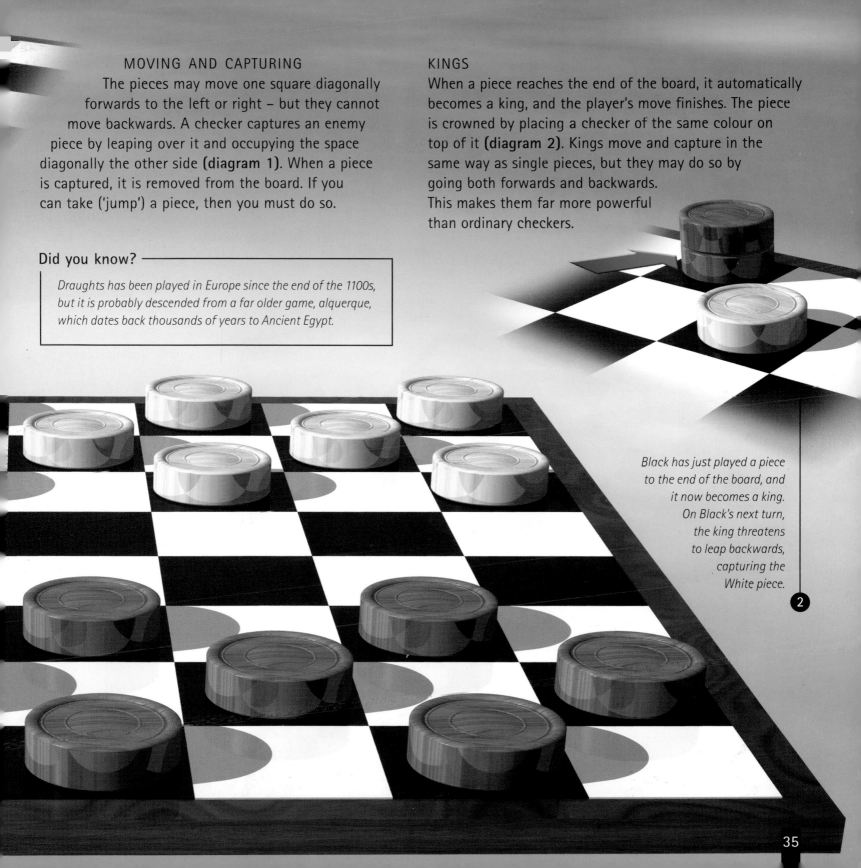

Black has just played a piece to the end of the board, and it now becomes a king. On Black's next turn, the king threatens to leap backwards, capturing the White piece.

2

White spots a serious weakness in Black's forces and finds a way to exploit it. White plays a piece forwards. According to the rules of the game, Black must capture.

1

TRICKS AND TRAPS

With its simple moves, you might think that draughts is a slow and straightforward game. In fact, danger lurks at every turn. One false move can lead to instant disaster, your forces crushed with no hope of a comeback.

The 'must capture' rule gives draughts its intrigue and complexity. It is the basis for some deadly traps, such as this example from early on in a game (diagrams 1–3).

2

Black's forced move sets up a spectacular series of leaps. White jumps over three of Black's checkers in one go. The move finishes at the end of the board, where White's piece becomes a king.

MIND THE GAP!
To avoid this kind of trap, some players keep the back checkers on their starting positions for as long as possible. This is a fair strategy, but it can be limiting – eventually the back checkers must move forwards to support the front pieces. Keeping a compact position is often a better tactic. As we have seen, leaving gaps between pieces can lead to disaster.

3

White gave up one piece, but captured three in return and gained a king. Such an advantage should be more than enough for White to win the game.

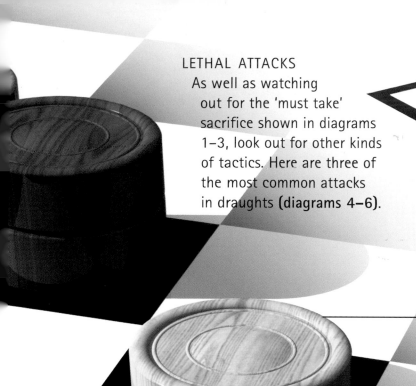

LETHAL ATTACKS

As well as watching out for the 'must take' sacrifice shown in diagrams 1–3, look out for other kinds of tactics. Here are three of the most common attacks in draughts (diagrams 4–6).

4 *THE FORK*
The Black king has just moved behind the two White pieces, attacking both. White can save one piece, but not both.

5 *INFILTRATION*
This is similar to the fork in that two pieces are attacked at the same time. In this case the attacker forces its way between the enemy checkers. White cannot avoid losing one piece.

DOMINATION
Be wary when playing your pieces to the side of the board, particularly at the end of a game. They will have more limited movement than on an open board, and could be dominated and trapped. In this example, the Black king's move helps to trap both of White's kings at the same time. The best White can do is give up one king to free the other. This leaves Black with two kings against one and a fairly simple win.

6

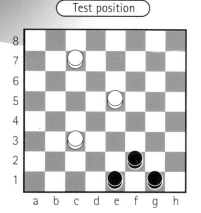

TEST POSITIONS

There are many subtle and beautiful finishes in draughts. Test your skill with the two problem positions below. The solutions are on pages 60–61.

Test position

(White is playing down the board. Black to play and win)

Black has a neat way of forcing White to self-destruct in this position. You need to think ahead for several moves to solve this problem.

Test position

(White is playing down the board. Black to play and win)

With a piece close to becoming a king, White appears to have good chances to win. But Black finds an unexpected way to turn the game. Think ahead for several moves to find the solution.

▲ *These playing cards from the Ottoman Empire are the direct ancestors of our modern packs. Ottoman packs also contained 52 cards and four suits. They came to Europe along trade routes through Spain and Italy.*

▲ *No one knows when and where playing cards first appeared, but Chinese money cards certainly existed before European cards. The four Chinese suits were coins, strings, myriads and tens. The designs on the cards were copied from paper money notes of the Tang Dynasty (CE 618–907).*

INTRODUCTION

Playing cards first arrived in Europe in the 1370s, from the Middle East. Card games spread rapidly throughout the continent. By the 15th century, the craze for cards was well-established among all levels of society.

WORD OF MOUTH

Card games are true folk games. In other words, they are generally spread by word of mouth – between family generations, for example. This accounts for the considerable variation in rules for many card games. Even when the 'standard version' of a game is written down, it rarely survives in that state for very long. That applies to this book too. If you think you can improve on the rules for the games given here, then do so.

◀ *A European king and his courtiers enjoy a game of cards in this illustration from a medieval manuscript.*

Tip

All the card games described in this book are played with a standard 52-card pack.

FRENCH SUITS AND COURT CARDS

The 52-card pack that is standard in the English-speaking world – and increasingly internationally – derives from France. It features the so-called French suits of clubs, diamonds, hearts and spades. The designs date back to medieval times, and have hardly changed in 500 years.

The king, queen and jack are known as 'court cards' or 'picture cards'. To modern eyes, the designs look rather rough. They were originally printed from woodcuts, and the same pictures have remained to the present day. The origin of king and queen is clear, but the jack is less obvious. This card was originally known as the 'knave' (a male servant). When letters came to be written on the cards to aid identification, it was too confusing to have 'K' for king and 'Kn' for knave. Another name for the card took over – 'Jack', one of the most common names at that time.

▼ The jack, queen and king are known as court cards. In most games, court cards are highly ranked.

▼ Until the 19th century, playing cards had no numbers or letters to identify them. These French cards date from 1752. The flat look of the characters is very similar to that of modern-day court cards.

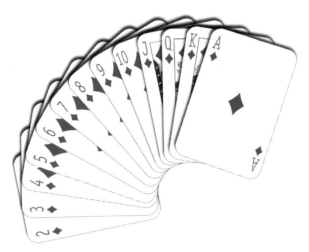

▲ *The suit of diamonds in order of rank. The ace is usually ranked the highest, with the 2 (also known as the deuce) being the lowest. The word 'ace' derives from the Latin word as – a small unit of coinage.*

THE PACK

The standard pack has 52 cards in four different suits. There are two red suits – hearts and diamonds – and two black suits – clubs and spades. The 13 cards in each suit are usually ranked from 2 (lowest) to ace (highest), but take care, because in some games the ace ranks as the lowest card.

In most card games, certain routines are followed to demonstrate that play is fair. While most people wouldn't dream of cheating, it is still important to carry out these procedures. They make everyone feel comfortable, and lend the game some ceremony.

SHUFFLING AND CUTTING
Before dealing a new round of cards, it is customary to shuffle and cut the cards. Shuffling ensures that players do not receive similar cards, and that the cards have not been placed in a particular order beforehand. Then the player sitting to the right of the dealer cuts the pack in two by lifting off roughly half the cards and placing them on the table. The dealer then places the lower half of the pack on top. When shuffling, the bottom card of the pack is often visible. Cutting ensures that the bottom card remains unknown.

DEALING
Cards are generally dealt face down, one at a time, in a clockwise direction, beginning with the player to the dealer's left. No cards should be picked up from the table until all the cards have been dealt. This makes it easier for the dealer to see how many cards have been given to each player.

▲ *Many countries have unique packs of cards, often with fewer than 52 cards and with different suits. These Venetian cards, from 1758, feature cups, swords, coins and cudgels.*

HOLDING THE CARDS

When the correct number of cards has been dealt, players may pick them up. First, arrange your cards so that you can see what you hold at a glance. For games like whist, hearts and spades, it is best to divide the cards into their suits. Within the suits, place cards in order of rank. Alternate red and black suits to avoid confusion.

Always ensure that none of the other players can see your hand. Hold your cards up, keeping them in a tight fan. Once you have arranged the cards in order, close them in a single pack in your hand, then fan them out again by spreading the back cards underneath the top one.

LEARNING THE RULES

At first glance, the rules of card games can seem baffling. Don't worry! The best way to learn the games described in this book is to take a pack of cards and play a practice game as you read – either on your own or with a friend. You will soon gain the confidence to begin playing for real.

▲ *This 13-card hand has been arranged into alternating suits, with cards placed in order of rank.*

▼ *Parisian card-makers at work in 1680. At the time, many governments imposed a tax on every pack of cards that was manufactured.*

▲ *Card games can be picked up from an early age. As well as being great fun, they are a great way to test your memory and use your maths.*

Did you know?

Many expressions from card games have entered everyday language. If someone is described as 'playing his cards close to his chest', it means he gives little away about his plans.

◄ *Ganjifa is the national card game of India. The cards are usually round. These particular cards, dating back around 200 years, are made of ivory.*

FIRST CARD GAMES

Player three

Playing these simple and entertaining games will help reinforce your knowledge of the card rankings. They are also useful stepping stones to the games that follow.

Player two

▼ *Here, player one is about to lay a 5. The first player to shout 'snap!' will win all three piles of upturned cards.*

SNAP

The aim of this game for two or more players is to win all the cards.

The cards are divided equally between the players. Players do not look at their cards, but place them in a face-down pile called a deck. The player to left of the dealer turns over one card and starts a face-up pile beside his deck. The next player to the left does the same, and so on, around the table. If two cards match, such as two jacks or two 3s, the first player to shout 'snap!' wins all the upturned cards. Play then continues with the player to the left of the last person to turn over a card.

If a player uses up all his cards, he forms a new deck with his upturned cards. A player who loses all his cards is out of the game. If snap is called incorrectly, that player must give a card to each of the other players.

Speed snap is played in the same way, but the players turn over their cards simultaneously.

Player one

► *Easy snap is a game for two players. The pack is divided and the cards are then played in turn on to a central pile. If the top two cards match, shout 'snap!' or slap your hand down on the pile. The game works best if several sets are removed from the pack (all 2s, 3s, 4s, 5s, 6s and 7s, for example). This increases the chance of matching cards.*

Player two   **Player one**

CUCKOO

In this game for three or more players, the aim is to avoid being left with the lowest card. The cards rank from king (highest) to ace (lowest). Each player has three lives at the start of play.

Each player is dealt one card. Players look at their card without letting it be seen by the others. The player to the left of the dealer decides whether to keep or exchange the card. If the card is high, he should keep it. Otherwise, he puts the card face down on the table and gives it to the player to his left, saying 'change'.

The next player can refuse to exchange if his card is a king, in which case the first player must keep his own card. But if not, he must exchange. Now player two decides whether to keep or exchange with the person to his left. When it is the dealer's turn, if he wishes to exchange, he cuts the pack and takes the top card from the lower half. If the card is a king, he loses the round and a life.

► *After the exchanges, the players show their cards. The player with the lowest card loses a life. Here, players five and six tie for lowest card, so they both lose a life. Because player five has lost his third life, he drops out. The last player left in the game is the winner.*

Player five

Player four

Player six

Player three

Player one

Player two

RUMMY

Rummy became popular in America around 100 years ago, and was taken up by many people working in the Hollywood movie industry. It was an ideal game to play during breaks in filming, as hands can be fast-moving.

THE AIM

The aim in rummy is to get rid of all your cards by melding. A meld is a set of three or more cards – either three or four of a kind, or a run of three or more cards of the same suit in rank order **(diagram 1)**. Aces are low, so the lowest possible run is A-2-3. The highest is J-Q-K.

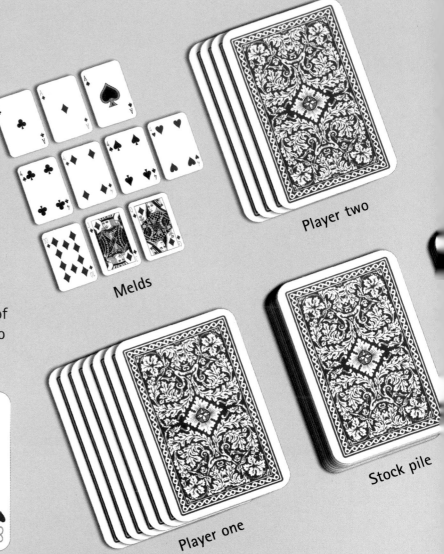

Player two

Melds

Stock pile

Player one

1 *Two examples of a meld in rummy – three of a kind (left) and a run of three hearts (right).*

THE DEAL

For a two-player game of rummy, deal ten cards each. For three to five players, deal seven cards each. For six players, deal six cards each. The remaining cards are placed face down to make the stock pile. The top card is turned up and placed next to the stock pile to form the discard pile.

CARD PLAY

The player to the left of the dealer begins. He takes either the top card from the stock pile, or the upturned card from the discard pile. If he has any melds, he may lay them down. On later turns, he may lay off single cards on to any existing melds on the table. A player can make as many melds and lay-offs in one turn as he wishes. Finally, the player adds a card to the discard pile. (Note – if you take a card from the discard pile, you cannot put the same card back.) The turn then passes to the next player to the left.

If the stock pile runs out, turn over the discards to form a new stock. Turn the top card over to make a new discard pile. The players decide whether to shuffle the stock pile or not. Leave the cards if you want to test your memory, shuffle them if you like the game to be more random.

WINNING AND SCORING

The player who gets rid of his last card – either by creating a new meld, by laying off, or by a discard – wins the round (diagram 2). His score is the total value of the cards held by the other players. Aces count as one, court cards all score ten, and the others have their face value (diagram 3). If a player lays down his entire hand in one turn, he scores double for a 'rummy'. After scoring, the deal passes to the next player for a new round. Play continues until an agreed points total, such as 200, has been reached.

Player two (24 points)

Discard pile

Player three

Player four

Player one (45 points)

Player three (25 points)

Melds

3 *After player four discards his last card, the other players reveal their hands. Player one has 45 points, player two has 24 points, and player three, 25 points. Player four's total score for the round is 94 points.*

2 *Here, player four seizes his chance by taking the 8 of clubs from the discard pile. He forms a meld with the 7, 8 and 9 of clubs, lays off the ace of hearts on the meld of three aces and, finally, discards the king of spades. He has no cards left, so the round is over.*

Tips

- *If you have a meld, you do not have to lay it down immediately – that might allow your opponents to lay off cards. Don't hang on to melds for too long, however – you might be caught with the cards if someone goes out.*
- *In general, discard higher scoring cards and keep lower ones. Even if you don't win the round, at least you won't give too many points to your opponents.*

CRIBBAGE

The English game of cribbage dates back to the 1600s. Once the rules are mastered, it is simple, but to play well you need a sharp eye to spot scoring opportunities. Points are won with card play, and the scores marked out with pegs on a special cribbage board. You can keep score with a pen and paper if you don't have a board.

Cribbage is a two-player game in which the aim is to reach 121 points. The cards have the usual ranking, except that the ace is low. Each card has a numerical value – all picture cards score ten, and the rest have their face value, including the ace, which scores one. These values become important when playing the cards and scoring. Diagram 1 shows how to set up at the start of a game.

▲ *Cribbage was supposedly invented by Sir John Suckling, a 17th-century adventurer, poet and gambler, although it has its roots in earlier English games.*

Non-dealer

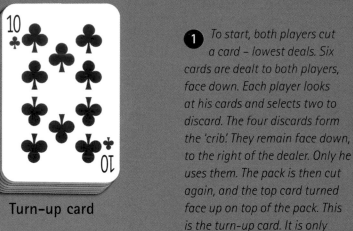

Turn-up card

Dealer

Crib

1 *To start, both players cut a card – lowest deals. Six cards are dealt to both players, face down. Each player looks at his cards and selects two to discard. The four discards form the 'crib'. They remain face down, to the right of the dealer. Only he uses them. The pack is then cut again, and the top card turned face up on top of the pack. This is the turn-up card. It is only used after the card play.*

Points are scored for card combinations in play with your opponent, and at the end of card play when hands are shown. The table on page 47 shows the various scoring combinations.

COMBINATION	EXAMPLE	SCORE
Fifteen (any group of cards totalling 15)		2 points
Pair (two cards of the same rank)		2 points
Pair royal (three cards of the same rank)		6 points
Double pair royal (four cards of the same rank)		12 points
Run (a sequence of at least three cards in rank order. Cards do not have to be the same suit)		1 point per card
Flush (any four or five cards of the same suit)		1 point per card

CARD PLAY

The non-dealer always begins. He lays one of his four cards face up on the table and announces its value. For example, if he lays a king he would say 'ten'. The dealer then plays a card, keeping it separate from his opponent's card. If he has a 5 he should lay it down, announcing 'fifteen for two points' – the total value of the cards laid so far and the number of points he receives. Watch out for any card combinations that score points. The players take turns to lay a card, each time announcing the running total and any scoring combinations.

If, by laying a card, one of the players hits a total of 31 points exactly, then he scores two points. If a player would exceed 31 points by laying his next card, he stops

playing and says 'go'. The opponent then continues laying cards until he either hits 31 (scoring two points), or he cannot play without bringing the total over 31. At that point, he announces 'go' and scores a point for playing the last card.

Whenever a player hits 31, or both players have announced 'go', the face-up cards are turned over and the game restarts with the remaining cards in each player's hand. The player who did not score at the end of the play leads. The count starts again at zero, with 31 again being the target. Players must keep their own cards on one side, even though they have already been played. They will be needed in the next part of the game.

47

SCORING AT THE SHOW

After the card play has finished, the players take back their own cards for the 'show'.

Each player turns his hand face up and announces all the scoring combinations. The non-dealer goes first. Both players use the 'turn-up card' to form combinations. After the dealer has announced the points scored from his hand, he does the same with the cards in the crib. When making combinations from the crib, there is one scoring exception – a flush can only be scored with five cards.

Diagrams 1 and 2 illustrate the scoring at the show, using the same cards dealt out on page 46.

1 *The non-dealer has three scoring combinations – a pair and two runs. The total score for his hand is eight points.*

Pair (2 points)

Three-card run (3 points)   Three-card run (3 points)

Dealer's hand | **Crib**

 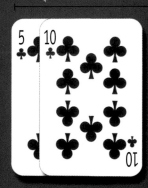   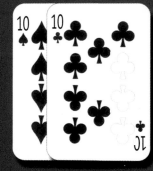

Pair (2 points)   Fifteen (2 points)   Fifteen (2 points)   Fifteen (2 points)   Pair (2 points)

2 *The dealer's hand has one scoring combination – a pair. The crib gives him three fifteens and a pair. The dealer's total score for the round is ten points – the combined scores of his own hand and the crib.*

BONUS POINTS

If the turn-up card is a jack, the dealer scores two bonus points. This must be scored before any cards are played. If either player has a jack of the same suit as the turn-up card, then he scores one bonus point. This should not be announced until the show.

STRATEGY

The skill in cribbage lies in maximizing your scoring opportunities while minimizing your opponent's. Following the tips below might not work out every time, but the odds will be in your favour.

If you are the dealer, put strong cards into the crib, but at the same time keep cards in your hand that offer good chances to score. It's not easy to do both, so if in doubt, favour the crib with the best cards, such as:

- two 5s
- 4 and an ace
- 5 and a card worth ten
- 5 and 6
- 6 and 9
- 2 and 3
- 7 and 8
- any pair

In the crib, these cards offer scoring opportunities such as fifteen for two points, or a pair for two points.

▼ A cribbage board keeps track of the game's stop-start scoring. Each player has two pegs. Here, Black has already scored six points, as shown by the position of the front peg in the sixth hole. If Black now scores eight points from card play, he counts eight holes ahead of the front peg and places the back peg there. The back peg is always used for counting, while the front peg marks the total score so far. Pegs are played up the outer rows of holes, then down the inner rows. The player who reaches the game hole after two circuits of the board (i.e. scores 121 points) is the winner.

Black's front peg

Black's back peg

Game hole

If you are the non-dealer, lay cards into the crib that do not help with scoring. It would be a mistake to put a 5 into the crib, as it could be combined with a card worth ten to make fifteen. Do not discard cards that are close together in rank, such as a 7 and a 9 – if the dealer puts an 8 into the crib, a run is formed. So the best cards for the non-dealer to lay in the crib are those far apart, such as a 2 and a 9, or a king and a 3.

When playing the first card, avoid laying a 5 – there is a high chance that your opponent could have a card worth ten, making the total score fifteen and gaining two points.

WHIST

Whist is a great game in itself, but it also forms the basis of many other popular card games. If you can play whist, you have made the first step towards games such as hearts and spades (pages 52–55), and the complexity of bridge.

THE DEAL

Whist is a game for four players, two playing against two as partners. The usual rankings apply, with aces counting high. Thirteen cards are dealt out face down to each player (diagram 1). The last card is turned up to show trumps for that hand (i.e. if the last card is the 10 of diamonds, then diamonds would be trumps). The dealer leaves this card on the table until the first trick has been played. The object of the game for both partnerships is to win the most tricks.

1 *In a game of whist, partners sit opposite each other. Players are named after the points of the compass, with North and South playing against East and West.*

North

East

West

South

TRICKS

A trick is a round of cards made up of one card per player. To win a trick, you have to play the highest card in that round. Each player has 13 cards, so there are 13 tricks in each hand. Diagram 2 shows how the first trick might be played.

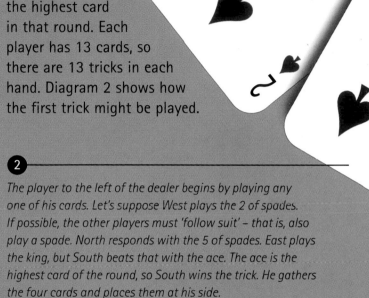

2

The player to the left of the dealer begins by playing any one of his cards. Let's suppose West plays the 2 of spades. If possible, the other players must 'follow suit' – that is, also play a spade. North responds with the 5 of spades. East plays the king, but South beats that with the ace. The ace is the highest card of the round, so South wins the trick. He gathers the four cards and places them at his side.

3 *Carrying on with the game, the winner of the last trick, South, must lead. He plays the queen of spades, but is unlucky. As West has no spades left, he cannot follow suit, and is allowed to lay any other card. He plays a trump card, the 3 of diamonds. The other players have to follow suit – the 7 of spades (North) and the 3 of spades (East). West wins the trick with the 3 of diamonds.*

TRUMPS

One thing upsets the usual ranking order – trumps. In the hand shown in diagram 1, let's suppose that diamonds are trumps. Every single diamond then ranks higher than any card from another suit. Diagram 3 illustrates how trump cards make the game more unpredictable.

SCORING

There are several ways of scoring, but the so-called American version is the simplest. In a hand, the first six tricks won by a partnership do not score. After this, each trick scores one point. So a partnership winning eight tricks would score two points. The first side to seven points wins a game, and the first side to win two games wins the match. Partners who revoke (do not follow suit when they are able to do so) must give the opposition two points.

SPADES

Spades is very popular in North America. It is a true folk game, in that there is no definitive version – so make sure that all four players are clear about the rules before beginning a game.

THE DEAL

The set-up is almost the same as in whist, with four players in two partnerships. Partners sit opposite each other, and 13 cards are dealt to each player. Aces rank high, and spades are always trumps.

BIDDING

First, the members of the non-dealer partnership discuss how many tricks they think they can win between them. They must not reveal anything about their hands, except the number of tricks each player thinks he might win on his own. When the partnership has agreed on a total number of tricks, it is written down. This is their contract. Then the dealer's team does the same.

A player who thinks he can lose every trick may declare 'nil'. His partner then says how many tricks he can win (two nil bids are not allowed). The contract is lost if the nil-bidder wins any tricks.

A 'blind nil' bid is highly risky. Again, you must try not to win any tricks, but the bid must be made before looking at your cards. After examining them, you may exchange two cards with your partner. This bid can only be made if your team is at least 100 points behind.

◀ *A typical nil-bid hand. High cards, such as the king of diamonds and the 10 and jack of hearts, are covered by low cards of the same suit – so there is a good chance of not winning any tricks.*

CARD PLAY

Card play is almost the same as in whist (see pages 50–51), except that spades are always trumps. Spades cannot be led (played as the first card in a trick) until a spade has been played as a trump, or one player has only spades left.

SCORING

If a team wins the number of tricks they bid, they score ten times the bid, plus one point for each 'overtrick'. For example, if eight tricks were bid but nine were won, the score would be (8 x 10) + 1 = 81. Picking up overtricks is known as 'sandbagging'. There is a penalty for consistent sandbagging. If a side's number of overtricks reaches ten or more, 100 points is deducted from their score. The total number of overtricks is easy to see – it is the last digit of the score. So, a team with 368 points has collected eight overtricks. If on the next hand they were to bid five tricks but win nine, the four overtricks would bring them above ten. Their score would be 368 + 54 = 422. Deducting 100 points brings the score back to 322. The two extra 'sandbags' are carried over to the next cycle of ten. After the twentieth overtrick, another 100 points would be deducted.

For a failed contract, a side loses ten points per trick bid. So, if seven tricks are bid but only five are won, 70 points are deducted from the partnership's total score.

A successful nil bid scores 100 points, plus or minus what is won or lost from the partner's bid. If four tricks are bid and won, the score would be 140 points. If a nil bid fails, 100 points are deducted from the score, but any tricks taken by the nil-bidder count towards the partner's contract. Blind nil is the same, but doubled to 200 points.

The first team to reach an agreed points total – usually 250 or 500 – is the winner.

Test hand

Should you make a nil bid with this hand?

Test hand

How many tricks might you aim to win with this hand?

HEARTS

Hearts belongs to the same family of card games as whist and spades. It demands skill, but fortunes can change rapidly and unexpectedly. There is plenty of scope for devious strategy, so be alert. Different versions of the game are found all over the world – Black Maria is the popular name in Britain.

1 *Each heart is worth one penalty point, regardless of its face value. The queen of spades scores 13 penalty points.*

THE AIM

Card play and trick-taking are very similar to whist, but the aim of hearts is different. You must avoid winning tricks that contain hearts or the queen of spades, as these incur penalty points **(diagram 1)**. Alternatively, you can try to 'shoot the moon' – that is, win all 14 penalty cards. Hands are played until one player reaches an agreed number of points, such as 100. The winner is the player with the lowest score at that moment.

THE DEAL AND EXCHANGE

Four players are dealt 13 cards each. Aces rank high. Before play begins, each player selects any three cards from his hand and passes them face down to the player to the left. On the next deal, cards are passed to the right; on the deal after that, cards are exchanged between the players facing each other; and on the fourth deal, no cards are exchanged. The pattern then repeats itself.

CARD PLAY

Whoever holds the 2 of clubs plays it as the first card. Just like in whist, players must follow suit if possible. There are no trumps. Penalty cards cannot be played on the first trick, unless there is no alternative. Hearts can only be led once a heart has been thrown on another suit as a penalty point.

PENALTY POINTS

At the end of each hand, players add up the penalty points in the tricks they have won. If a player shoots the moon by winning all 14 penalty cards, he can either deduct 26 points from his score, or add 26 points to each of his opponents' scores. This is where the deviousness of the game comes in. It might appear that one player is doing badly, having picked up many penalty points. If he has a strong hand, however, he might aim to pick up all the penalty cards, landing his opponents with a huge score.

North

East

West

South

2 At the start of this hand, West creates a void by exchanging the 6 and king of clubs. This will make it easier to dump penalty points on his opponents. North and South pass on some of their high cards. East wisely exchanges the queen of spades.

STRATEGY

Selecting the right cards to exchange is crucial **(diagram 2)**. If you are dealt the queen of spades, should you pass it on, or keep it, hoping to give someone a nasty surprise later on?

- If you have the queen of spades plus just one other spade, it is best to exchange the queen – if you keep it, it could easily be forced out, and you might have to take the trick and the penalty points.

- If you have the queen of spades plus at least three other spades, it is usually safe to keep the queen. The other spades can be played when spades are led, and in the meantime you should have a chance to dump the queen on an opponent once a void (a lack of any cards in one suit) appears in your hand.

- Unless you want to shoot the moon, keep your 2s and 3s. Leading these usually ensures that someone else wins the trick. High cards can be useful too. The ace of hearts, for example, may stop an opponent from shooting the moon.

BLACKJACK

This betting game is known by several names, including pontoon, twenty-one and vingt-et-un. Each version has slightly different rules. Blackjack is the name of the casino version. The game described here is very near to that, and can be played at home – or anywhere else for that matter.

Blackjack is best with three or more players. Cards are worth their face value, with aces worth either one or eleven. The picture cards are all worth ten. The suits are irrelevant. Each player starts with a fixed number of chips, or counters – let's say 30 – for betting.

THE AIM
Players try to beat the dealer by ending up with cards whose total value is greater than his, but not more than 21.

THE DEAL
First, draw cards to decide who is dealer – lowest deals. Before the cards are dealt, each player bets the amount he wishes, but a maximum initial stake should be agreed beforehand. In diagram 1, each player has bet two chips. Then the dealer deals two cards face upwards to each player and then two to himself – one face up and the other face down.

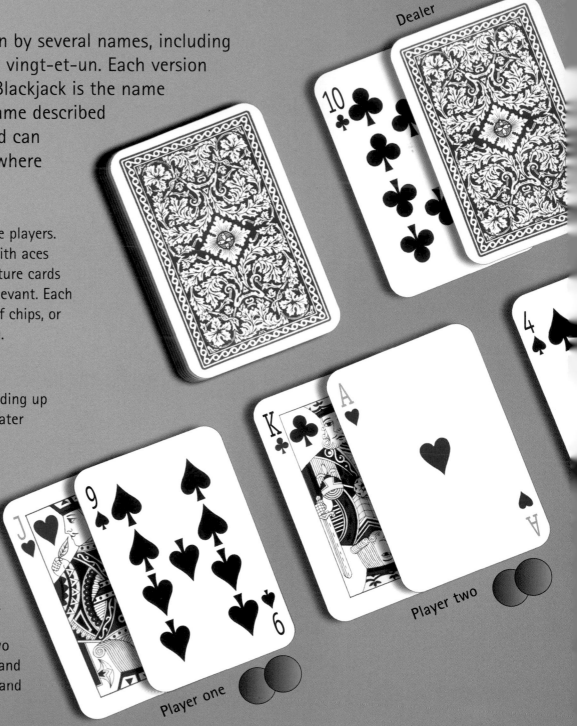

Dealer

Player one

Player two

STAND, DOUBLE, HIT OR SPLIT

At this point, a player has different options (diagrams 1 and 2):

- To stand (or 'stick') – that is, to ask for no more cards from the dealer.
- To double the original stake, but receive only one more card – a good bet if the cards total nine, ten or eleven. The odds of receiving a ten-card are strong, which would give a good score to stand on.

- To hit (or 'twist') – to be dealt an extra card face upwards, without increasing the stake. If a player's total goes above 21, he is 'bust' and his stake goes to the dealer.
- If a player has a pair, he may 'split' the cards, and play each as a separate hand. He must bet an additional stake, the same as the original stake, to cover the second hand.
- If a player has an ace and a card worth ten, he has a 'blackjack'. If the dealer's upturned card shows that he does not have a blackjack, he pays the player double his stake. If the dealer also has a blackjack, neither side wins – the player's stake is returned.

1 *Here, player one has 19 and decides to stand – the correct decision. Another card could take the total over 21. Player two has a blackjack. The dealer does not pay out yet, as he might also have a blackjack. Player three's cards total 12. He decides to hit – he receives a 2, bringing the total to 14. He hits again and gets a 10. The total is now 24, so he is bust. Player four has 11 and decides to double. He receives one extra card, an 8 – bringing the total to 19.*

Player four

Player three

Dealer

2 *At this point, the dealer turns up his face-down card – an 8. He stands on this score of 18. Now it is time to settle up. Player one beat the dealer with 19. He wins four chips (two from the dealer plus his initial stake of two). Player two wins double his stake for a blackjack. He receives six chips (four from the dealer plus his stake of two). Player three went bust, so loses his stake to the dealer. Player four doubled his initial stake to four and beat the dealer with 19. He wins eight chips in total.*

Player four

Player three

Player two

Player one

1 *Poker hands are ranked in a fixed order, from a royal flush (highest) to a pair (lowest). If players have none of these, the hand with the highest single card wins.*

Royal flush

Ace, king, queen, jack and 10 of the same suit.

Straight flush

Five cards of the same suit, in rank order.

Four of a kind

Four cards of the same rank.

Full house

Three of a kind, plus a pair.

Flush

Five cards of the same suit, in any order.

Straight

Five cards in rank order, regardless of suit.

Three of a kind

Three cards of the same rank.

Two pairs

Two sets of two cards of the same rank.

One pair

Two cards of the same rank.

POKER

Poker is the card game of America. It is about bluff, bravery and cunning. Everyone has a chance to come from nothing and win a fortune through skill, luck and perseverance.

DRAW POKER
There are many different poker games – Crazy Pineapple, London Lowball, Skinny Minnie and Spit in the Ocean are just a few. The classic game of five-card draw poker is most often played. Five cards are dealt to between two and eight people, then players bet on who has the best hand. Hands are ranked in a fixed order (diagram 1).

SETTING UP
Before cards are dealt, everyone pays an 'ante' – an agreed starting bet. Decide also on the betting system. You can play 'limit', in which bets are fixed – at two chips, for example. With 'pot limit', you cannot bet more than the amount already in the pot. Or you can play 'no limit', in which you can bet as many chips as you have on the table. The example hand shown in diagrams 2 and 3 is pot limit.

Betting options

Check – to not make a bet. This is only possible if no bets have been made in that round.

Raise – to bet more than the previous player.

Call – to match the previous bet.

Call and raise – to match the previous bet and then increase the stakes again.

Player one

Player two

Player three

Pot

2 Here, the three players have each paid an ante of one chip. Player one likes his pair of kings and raises one chip. Player two wants to continue in the hand, so he 'calls'. That means he matches player one's bet by adding one chip. Player three has two pairs and likes his hand a lot. He calls by adding one chip, and raises by six chips.

Players one and two must at least match player three's bet if they want to continue in the hand. They call by each adding six chips to the pot. All three players have now wagered the same amount (eight each), so the next phase of the game begins – the draw. Each player may now exchange any number of cards with the dealer. Player one trades three cards, player two trades one card, and player three also trades one card.

After the exchanges, player one has not **3** improved his hand – he still has a pair of kings. He checks. That means he does not bet anything, but stays in the hand and keeps his options open. Player two has a flush. He raises by ten chips. Player three has not improved on two pairs, but is confident enough to stay in. He calls, adding ten chips to match player two's bet. There are now 44 chips in the pot.

Back to player one. To stay in the hand, he must add another ten chips. Is it worth it? Are the other two players bluffing? Not both of them! He decides not to take a risk and drops out.

The amount wagered by players two and three is now even, so the betting ends. It is time for the showdown. Player two wins the pot, as his flush beats player three's two pairs.

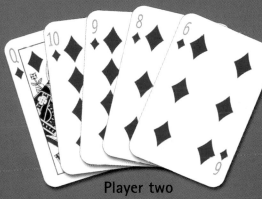

Player one

Player two

Pot

Player three

ANSWERS AND RESOURCES

GO TEST POSITION, PAGE 23

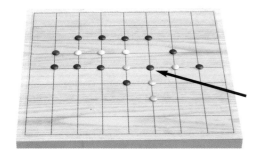

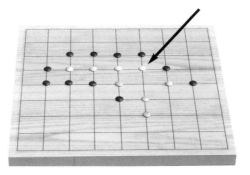

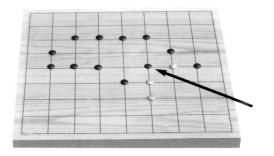

1 *Black occupies the cutting point, and threatens to capture four White stones.*

2 *White captures one Black stone, but Black has the final word...*

3 *Black plays a stone on to the eye in the middle of White's formation. The group of five White stones has been surrounded. They are removed from the board.*

CHESS TEST POSITIONS, PAGE 29

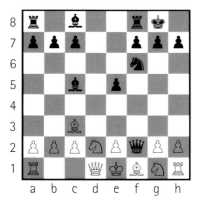

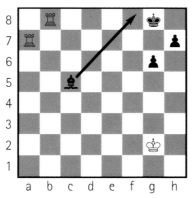

This is checkmate. White has lost the game.

This is not checkmate. Black can block the check from the rook by retreating the bishop to the f8 square.

MANCALA TEST POSITIONS, PAGE 33

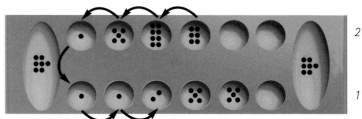

After sowing, player two will capture all the beans from the last three pots – seven in total.

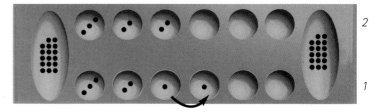

This modest move is the only way for player one to prevent player two capturing any beans. The outcome of the game remains open.

DRAUGHTS TEST POSITIONS, PAGE 37

Starting position

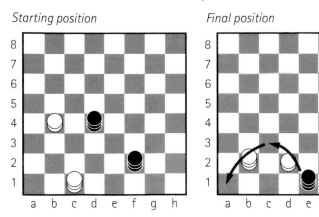

Final position

Starting position

Final position

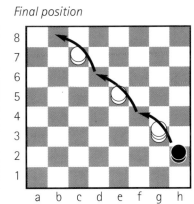

First, Black moves from d4 to c3. White must capture – b4 to d2. Then Black blocks with f2 to e1. White has only one move – c1 to b2, after which Black captures both pieces. Black wins the game.

First, Black gives away a piece – e1 to d2. White must capture, and in so doing gains a king – c3 to e1. Then Black gives away another piece – g1 to h2. White captures with e1 to g3. This lines up the pieces perfectly for Black to swoop down and take all White's pieces – h2 to b8. Game over!

SPADES TEST HANDS, PAGE 53

It is too risky to make a nil bid. The king of spades could easily win a trick, as could one of the clubs. There are no low cards in that suit to provide cover.

You could expect to win three tricks with this hand. Count one trick for the ace of hearts, one trick for either the king or queen of diamonds, and one trick for one of the four spade trumps.

THE INTERNET

There are several multi-game websites on the Internet where you can play most of the board and card games described in this book, in real time. Try the **www.yahoo.com** games site, or **www.zone.com** on MSN.

Many sites are dedicated to one particular game. These specialist sites often attract the real experts – and others too! For example, the premier chess-playing website is the Internet Chess Club at: **www.chessclub.com**. For backgammon, try **www.gamesgrid.com**.

You can play an online version of the champion draughts program Chinook at **www.cs.ualberta.ca/~chinook/**. Good practice before your next human opponent!

For a vast range of websites about go, start off at the International Go Federation: **www.world–go.org**. From there, you can find websites that feature online gaming, tutorials, tests, tournament information and contacts all over the world.

The best site for mancala is African Games: **www.myriadonline.com/awalink.htm**. Here, you can find information on the game's history, the rules of different versions, where to play online – against humans and computers, and links to other websites.

For card games, the best place to start is at **www.pagat.com**. This site lists card games from all over the world, and features rules, information and links to other sites.

GLOSSARY

BOARD GAMES

BACKGAMMON

Anchor An important **point**, usually in the opponent's home board, occupied by two or more of your counters.

Back counters The two counters furthest from your **home board** at the start of the game.

Bar The central ridge between the two halves of the board. Captured counters are placed on the bar.

Bearing off Removing counters from the board at the end of the game. This can only happen if a player has brought all of his counters into the **home board**.

Blockade To restrict the movement of your opponent's counters by building **points**.

Blot A single, vulnerable piece.

Golden point (or **golden anchor**) The five-point.

Hit To capture a piece.

Home board (or **inner board**) The quarter of the board where a player **bears off** his counters.

Outer board The area outside the home boards.

Point Any of the 24 spikes where the counters are placed.

'Making a point' or 'building a point' means to move two pieces on to the same spike. This makes them safe from attack.

Prime A row of four or more **points** that are each occupied by at least two counters, thus forming a blockade.

Race A position where further **hits** are impossible, or very unlikely. The game's outcome merely depends on which player rolls the higher dice scores.

CHESS

Castling A special move in which both the king and a rook can leave their starting squares on the same turn.

Check A piece that directly attacks the king is said to 'give check' or put it 'in check'.

Checkmate The end of the game, when the king is put in **check** and cannot escape.

Diagonal A line of squares running obliquely across the board. Only the bishop and the queen are able to move along the diagonals.

Double check When two pieces put the **king** in **check** at the same time.

File The columns of squares that run up the board, denoted by the letters 'a' to 'h'.

Major piece A queen or a rook.

Minor piece A knight or a bishop.

Promotion When a pawn reaches the eighth rank and turns into a knight, a bishop, a rook or a queen. Because the queen is so powerful, other pieces are rarely selected.

Rank The rows of squares that run across the board, denoted by the numbers 1 to 8.

Resignation When a player gives up the game before checkmate occurs, knowing that defeat is inevitable.

Stalemate When a player cannot make any legal moves, but is not in check. The game ends as a draw.

DRAUGHTS

Endgame A phase of the game in which both sides have made a **king**.

Jump (or **leap**) To make a capture.

King A single piece becomes a king when it reaches the final row of the board. A king is able to move backwards and forwards.

King-row The final row of the board, where single pieces become **kings**.

GO

Atari When stones are threatened with capture, they are said to be in 'atari'.

Cutting point A point that, if occupied, could divide and weaken an opponent's **group** of stones.

Eye An unoccupied point in the middle of a **group** of stones.

Group Two or more stones, belonging to one player, in the same area. It is often difficult to say whether a group is weak or strong. A group that has two **eyes** is safe from capture.

Intersection The point where two lines cross. Stones are placed on these points.

Komi Points (usually five and a half) added to White's score as compensation for Black having the first move. This is an optional rule.

Liberty An unoccupied point lying directly next to a stone, horizontally or vertically.

Wei-chi The Chinese word for go.

MANCALA

Sowing beans Moving pieces around the board.

Store hole Where captured beans are placed.

CARD GAMES

Ace high When the ace ranks as the highest card of a suit.

Ace low When the ace ranks as the lowest card of a suit.

Chip A gaming token.

Court card (or **picture card**) A king, queen or jack.

Cut To place the lower half of the pack on top of the upper half.

Deal To distribute cards to the players.

Deck A pack of cards.

Lead To play the first card.

Lead, the The first card played.

Turn-up card The top card of a pack, turned face-up and placed either on top of the pack or next to it.

BLACKJACK

Blackjack Two cards that total 21 – an ace plus a ten or a court card. A blackjack is sometimes known as a 'natural'.

Bust When a player's cards total more than 21, he is bust and loses his stake.

Double To double the original stake but receive just one more card – a good option if the two original cards total nine, ten or eleven.

Hit (or **twist**) To receive another card from the dealer.

Push A tie between dealer and player. The player takes back the original stake.

Split If you are dealt a pair, the cards can be split and played as two separate hands.

Stand (or **stick**) To decline to take another card from the dealer.

CRIBBAGE

Crib (or **box**) The hand of four cards formed by the discards of the players.

Flush Four or five cards that are all of the same suit.

Game hole The 121st hole on the cribbage board – the end of the game.

Go Said by a player when he cannot lay a card without the running total exceeding 31 points.

Run (or **sequence**) Three or more cards in rank order. The cards do not have to be of the same suit.

Show, the When the players take back their own cards and announce scoring combinations.

'Ten' cards The kings, queens, jacks and tens.

Thirty-one (**31**) When the running total of the cards played hits exactly 31, the player scores two points.

HEARTS

Break hearts To discard the first heart as a penalty point. Until a heart has been discarded, the heart suit cannot be **led**.

Shoot the moon To win all the penalty points.

POKER

Ante A compulsory bet placed by all the players before the deal.

Bluff To bet or raise with a poor hand in the hope that the other players will be scared off and **fold**.

Fold To throw in your hand.

Pot The total amount bet by the players.

Showdown The display of cards at the end of the hand.

RUMMY

Discard pile A pile made up of cards dumped by the players.

Lay off To add an individual card to an existing **meld**.

Meld A set of three or more cards – either three or four of a kind, or a run of at least three cards.

Run (or **sequence**) Three or more cards in rank order, all of the same suit.

Stock (or **stock pile**) The pile of undealt cards.

SPADES

Bid The declared number of **tricks** that a player expects to make.

Blind nil A nil **bid** declared before looking at the cards.

Break spades To lay the first spade as a **trump** card. Spades cannot be **led** until this happens.

Contract The number of **tricks** that a **partnership** aims to make.

Nil bid A player who makes a nil bid must avoid taking any **tricks**.

Overtricks **Tricks** made above the stated bid.

Sandbags Penalty points for **overtricks**. For every ten sandbags, 100 points is deducted from a **partnership's** score.

WHIST

Partnership Players sitting opposite who play together.

Revoke To fail to follow suit when able to do so, thus incurring a penalty.

Trick A round of cards, one from each player.

Trump To lay a trump card on a plain suit.

Trumps A superior suit. A card from the trump suit beats any card from another suit.

Void Having no cards in a suit.

INDEX